RENTAL SECRETS

Candi,
May you continue to
have a positive impact
on your audience.

Justin Tague

RENTAL SECRETS

Reduce Your Rent ~ Get Better Value

Create Quality Communities

Justin Pogue

Darpen
Belker
Press

First Edition: November 2018

Edited By:
Adam Guttentag
Jim Schibler

Cover Design:
James, GoOnWrite.com
Adam Guttentag

Paperback ISBN 978-1-54397-847-6
E-book ISBN 978-0-46-374835-0

Table of Contents

Dedication

This book is dedicated to my parents,
David and Stella, whose dedication,
support, and guidance laid the foundation
for all my achievements, both personal and
professional; and my sister Nicolette, who
is giving a similar foundation to my niece
Avery and nephew Julian.

Acknowledgements

Thank you to the dozens of people who assisted in creating this book. Whether you provided endorsements, constructive criticism, or helped with the title please know that your efforts however large or small are sincerely appreciated.

DISCLAIMER

This book is based on the author's personal experiences with and opinions about property management and rent price negotiation. The author is not licensed as an educational consultant, teacher, or real estate agent.

While best efforts have been used in preparing this book, the author and publisher are providing this book and its contents on an "as is" basis and make no representations or warranties of any kind with respect to this book or its contents. The author and publisher disclaim all such representations and warranties, including for example warranties of merchantability and educational, legal, accounting, or financial advice for a particular purpose. In addition, the author and publisher do not represent or warrant that the information accessible via this book is accurate, complete or current. Please consult with your own legal or accounting professional regarding the suggestions and recommendations made in this book.

Neither the author nor the publisher shall be held liable or responsible to any person or entity with respect to any loss, incidental or consequential damages caused, or alleged to have been caused, directly or indirectly, by the information or concepts contained herein. This is a comprehensive limitation of liability that applies to all damages of any kind, including (without limitation) compensatory; direct, indirect or consequential damages; loss of data, income or profit; loss of or damage to property and claims of third parties.

You understand that this book is not intended as a substitute for consultation with a licensed educational, legal, financial, or accounting professional. Every individual and situation is different and the advice and strategies contained herein may not be suitable for your situation. You should seek the services of a competent professional before signing any legal document. This book provides content related to legal, accounting, and financial topics. As such, use of this book implies your acceptance of this disclaimer.

Who Are These Secrets For?

This book is for anyone who currently lives in a rental home or is looking to do so. It is also for landlords, to help them think creatively about their relationship with their residents.

In addition, this book speaks to those who believe they have no control over their life and those who struggle to implement some control in their lives.

The secrets described herein are the numerous sources of power that regular, ordinary individuals have to affect how much they pay for rent. These secrets are hidden in plain sight and available for anyone to use. It is my goal to shed light on the possibility of using these powers to exert some control on the cost of rent. However, being aware of the possibility and making it a reality are two different things. Therefore, the strategies in this book are both concrete and actionable, resonating with both residents and landlords alike.

Why is the title "Rental Secrets: Reduce Your Rent, Get Better Value, and Create Quality Communities"? Both residents and landlords leave value on the table because they fail to realize they are partners in maintaining the quality communities we all deserve. The mainstream narrative places usurious, uncaring landlords at odds with overly-demanding, destructive residents. Both groups should be interested in creating value for each other. What does that look like? What ideas should renters think about as they reach out to landlords? How can landlords think about providing residents with the best deals they can? That is what this book is all about.

Your "Rental Secrets" are waiting for you. So let's get started!

Justin Pogue

Introduction

**Rental Empowerment
Loading...**

You have the power to get a better deal on the next property lease you sign.

Since my real estate career began in 2003, I have seen tried and true strategies that people have used to rent apartments for less than the annual average rent for their target area.

> - Do these people have special connections?

> - Are they using government programs like Section 8?

> - Did they convince the local church to pay their rent?

> - Are they renting properties that are falling apart?

> - Do they live in a slum?

You may be surprised to learn that the answer to all of these questions is "Absolutely not!" None of these strategies involve knowing the right people or braving government red tape. They don't require you to accept charity or live in less than acceptable conditions.

They do require knowing specifically what you want and need. Some strategies require research and leg work. But most of all they require developing an understanding of the landlord's predicament.

What landlord's predicament?

As a prospective resident seeking below market rent, you must understand that landlords have problems too. Contrary to what many believe, not all landlords are wealthy people. Most of the wealth landlords have is in the value of their buildings, not in liquid cash. They cannot simply walk up to a wall of their building and ask for $20. The most important thing their building does is create monthly cash flow from rent. The effort involved to ensure that this cash flow is steady and consistent, with little fluctuation can be a daunting, stressful task.

If you have ever been an employee, you expected your paycheck to be delivered on time, like clockwork. You plan your bills and vacations around receiving these payments. Imagine if your employer was less than reliable and the timing of your paycheck fluctuated. That would make your life more stressful and you would likely start looking for another job. Since landlords have mortgages and other expenses to pay to keep the property running, they feel the same way about receiving rent as you feel about receiving your paycheck.

The rental industry is based on providing a time-based service in exchange for money. For example, the longer you are in an apartment, the more money the landlord makes. If the apartment is vacant, the landlord makes no money. And it gets worse; the landlord really has no ability to ever earn back the money lost on a vacant apartment. If you owned a car dealership and you didn't sell a particular car today, you can sell it tomorrow. In the apartment game, that day of vacancy from last week can never be sold again – it is gone forever!

This reality constantly pushes landlords toward a bias for taking immediate action.

How does this create power for you?

You may think you don't have power, but you have more than you know. Your power comes from working with landlords who can negotiate. It comes from living on the property. Power flows from your market timing. It comes from keeping your situation simple. Your power comes from knowing how to maintain great relationships. Another source of power is being crystal clear on what you want. An additional source of power is asking questions, and one last source of power is having some basic accounting knowledge.

Using these powers, you have the ability to reduce the riskiness of the landlord's rent cash flows, help ensure the property is a great place to live, and get the best value for your money. And yes, the landlord will pay you for helping in these ways with lower rent. All of the strategies shown below create a win for you and a win for the landlord. This is why they are effective. The key is to recognize why you have power in the resident landlord relationship.

To effectively leverage these powers, it is important to understand how each one works. Not all of these strategies will work in every case, but fortune favors the bold and those with the knowledge to negotiate in ways that make landlords take notice. I have worked in major metropolitan markets like New York and Silicon Valley as well as smaller markets in Georgia and Mississippi. Landlords everywhere have many of the same issues and the same is true for renters. I have seen these strategies applied at one time or another in every market I have worked in. While I can't guarantee free rent, using these strategies can get you a better deal than you would receive otherwise. So let's get you full access to the power you have.

Chapter 1:
The Power of
Negotiation

You may have heard the statistic that 90% of millionaires became wealthy by investing in real estate. These investors come in all shapes and sizes. As a prospective resident looking for lower rent, there is a specific type of investor you are looking for. The investor you want is one who owns fewer than 100 apartments and works as their own property manager.

When working with self-managing landlords, you are working with someone empowered to make deals. Larger investors hire property management companies in an effort to avoid dealing with individual residents. While some property management companies have leeway to negotiate, most do not. Therefore, any negotiation would require them to go get approval from the property owner. But, the property owner specifically hired the property management company to handle their properties. No management company calls the property owner unless they really have to.

In addition, smaller investors are more motivated to negotiate. Larger investors can even out the fluctuations in their cash flow situation because their income is averaged out over hundreds, if not thousands of apartments. Consider an investor who owns one single family house. The property is either rented or it isn't. There is no middle ground between rented and 100% vacancy. Rented means there is income, vacancy means no income. If you offer to rent for $25 to $50 below their asking price per month, you just saved $300 - $600 per year. This can and does happen, especially if the property has been vacant for any length of time. Most landlords have mortgages and the monthly payments on those mortgages don't stop just because the property is vacant.

Property managers work with all types of residents from all walks of life and varied employment backgrounds. Their responsibilities include not only leasing to new residents, but also renewing the leases of those who are already residents. But, working on a renewal for a resident who works as a real estate journalist for the local business newspaper definitely adds a new twist. In this situation, the initial renewal offer included an increase of $100 per month based on the manager's analysis of the market in the apartment community's neighborhood.

This resident gathered data from properties outside the neighborhood and presented a number of viable, comparable alternatives. Not only were these alternatives less expensive than the renewal offer he'd received, they were cheaper than his current rent. Since the resident had substitutes that were readily available it made the possibility of losing the resident much more real. Armed with market data, and a stellar rent payment history, he created a strong bargaining position for himself. In the end, the resident and property manager settled on a smaller increase at $50 per month. The manager secured an increase and kept a current resident, avoiding vacancy and other apartment turnover costs. The resident avoided the cost and hassle of moving while saving $600 a year. For those keeping score, that's one to three extra car payments depending on what you drive.

If you are not a real estate journalist, you may be wondering how to find this information and why this would have credibility with your landlord. Perform an internet search for rental properties in your city. Numerous websites will appear that can help you locate suitable alternative properties, including Craigslist. While those websites will show pricing information it is best to confirm by calling the leasing associate for each property. The phone number should be available on your website of choice. Once armed with that information, your credibility is actually enhanced three ways. First, you are a resident who is currently deciding whether to renew or not. More specifically, you are deciding whether to maintain the continuity of the landlord's cash flow. Second, the pricing information you've discovered is real, verifiable, and relevant to your renewal decision. Third, the fact that you bothered to get the information shows just how serious you are.

There are a couple of factors that can enhance your power to negotiate. First, focus on smaller investors who self-manage to be sure they can negotiate, or work with property managers who have at least some leeway to negotiate. Second, you don't need to be a real estate journalist - just look for pricing information from other communities to support your negotiation position. Working with those who can negotiate and having actual market information at your side makes the power of negotiation the most effective.

The Power of Negotiation

SUMMARY

❖ Seek out rental properties where you can work directly with managers empowered to negotiate, whether they are an owner or a property manager.

❖ The fewer rental properties someone owns the higher the impact of rental income fluctuations.

❖ The owner's mortgage doesn't stop just because the rental property is vacant.

The Power of Negotiation

QUESTIONS

❖ Self-managing owners own smaller properties. How would living in a smaller community be beneficial for you?

_____

_____

_____

_____

_____

_____

❖ Do you believe there would be any drawbacks to living in a smaller community?

_____

_____

_____

_____

_____

❖ Describe how having direct contact with the owner would be advantageous for you?

_____

_____

_____

_____

_____

_____

_____

Chapter 2:
The Power of
Competition

Property owners and property management companies define market competition very differently than you or I do. Therefore, when they say their rents are competitive it doesn't mean what the average person thinks it means. When these companies look at their competition, they perform a market analysis based on properties similar to their own. These properties are chosen based on their close proximity as well as having similar interior finishes, property condition, and amenities. They do this to simplify their market analysis and to compare apples to apples as best they can.

While this may sound very logical and reasonable, this method - while simple - leaves out options that a renter may very well consider. These options include single-family homes, smaller multi-family properties, or properties in other parts of the city. For example, you may live in an apartment complex 15 minutes east of where you work. You might consider an acceptable substitute to be a complex that is 15 minutes west of your job. Your current apartment complex likely does not factor that option into their market analysis. Their answer would be that those are not considered to be comparable properties. The question is, not considered comparable by whom? As the renter it is your choice to determine which options make sense for you, meaning any property you would consider is actually their competition.

So next time you hear "Our rents are competitive with the market" be sure to understand specifically what market they are referring to before you assume that information is correct. They believe that statement is true based on the "market analysis" they have done, but, understand that it is likely incomplete and certainly not matched to any specific resident's point of view.

If a property manager presents an unacceptable rental price to you, don't just complain that it's unacceptable. Show them who their competition really is from your perspective because they really may not know. This can be powerful both when choosing a new rental property or renewing the lease where you currently live.

There is an incredible array of rental choices available. It is extremely rare for a rental community to have no competition. Understand that competition between rental properties and apartment complexes can be quite intense. A simple internet search for rental property in your city will reveal just how many competitors are in your market. As you get deeper into your search, you will determine which of the competitors best meets your needs.

Each of these rental choices will work to establish themselves as the best value for you. One way they attempt to be the best value is to offer discounts or deals. These offers may include a reduced deposit, free rent for a specific number of weeks, rental discounts, or some combination thereof. It is important to note that some of these offers provide a benefit upfront and reduce the funds required to move-in. Other offers reduce the monthly cost of rent over the term of the lease. Therefore, it is important to be clear on which type of deal would be most beneficial for you.

You may be thinking that less money up front is always preferable. However, this is not the case. Landlords typically require proof of monthly income equal to 2.5 – 3 times the monthly rent amount. For example if the rent is $2000 per month, you would need to prove your income is between $5,000 and $6,000 per month. However, if their deal reduces the rent by $100 to $1,900 then the amount of income you'd need to prove would also drop. Knowing this information, you can determine whether you'd prefer to accept upfront discounts or spread the discount over the term of the lease to reduce the monthly rent to help you qualify.

If you're thinking that when your rent goes up in a year that you'll no longer qualify, you can relax. Landlords rarely if ever require you to requalify for a market-rate rental property you are already in. This is especially true if the occupants of the rental property don't change. In fact, once you are a resident, the most important factors become the quality of your payment history and your relationship with the landlord.

Standing out in a crowded apartment marketplace is difficult, so property managers will often use incentives. It can be even more difficult for newly built properties to attract attention so many of them actually offer free rent. Free rent is not a fairytale. It is a specific marketing strategy used by many apartment communities to stand out from the crowd.

During the entire construction phase, new buildings cannot collect any rent. All real estate is essentially useless until a certificate of occupancy is received from the city or county it is located in. Of course, they will attempt to convince people to leave a deposit to lock down an apartment in the "hippest new community in the area". But, this is difficult to do with no completed apartments to show. But more importantly, a deposit is not rental income. The property manager cannot, by law, use those funds to pay their expenses. That money actually still belongs to the person who left the deposit. The property manager just gets to hold it.

For example, a newly constructed apartment community in the San Francisco Bay Area offered 6 weeks of free rent in order to stand out and attract new residents. This offer equated to approximately $4,500 in value. In addition, they paid someone to wave a sign proclaiming their offer at the closest intersection. This type of advertising is not cheap. A "human directional" (Yeah, I never liked that term either) as they are called in the advertising world, can cost over $1,000 per week for just a few hours each day. This is just one example of a real life offer of free rent. Craigslist is a fantastic place to search for similar offers in your area quickly and efficiently.

The key is to understand that rental properties and apartment communities are all competing against each other. You may find a particular deal at one community that your preferred community is not offering. Ask the leasing agent or the property manager if you can get that deal at their community. You never know what pressures, deadlines, or goals that community might be dealing with. Remember, you are their customer and they don't make any money until a customer signs a lease.

The Power of Competition

SUMMARY

❖ The property management company's list of competitors likely differs from your list of comparable, substitute apartment communities.

❖ When working with property management, present evidence of what your alternatives are.

❖ Be clear on which discounts & incentives would be most helpful for you.

The Power of Competition

QUESTIONS

❖ Which areas of your city meet your livability criteria?

_____

_____

_____

_____

_____

_____

❖ Which communities in each of those areas would you view as acceptable substitutes?

_____

_____

_____

_____

_____

_____

❖ Would weeks of free rent, a lower deposit, or lower monthly rent for the term of the lease be best for you?

_____

_____

_____

_____

_____

_____

_____

Chapter 3:
The Power of
Proximity

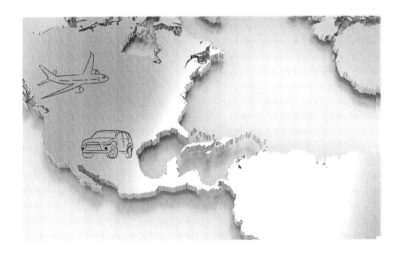

Out-of-town owners are in a stressful situation. They are renting their property to prospective residents they may only have met once. Their ability to drive by and check up on the property is hampered by distance. They are typically too far away to do any maintenance or repairs themselves so they are forced to hire outside professionals. Just having a licensed plumber or contractor arrive at the property could cost $100 or more. And what's more, these issues are just the tip of the iceberg.

You may be asking "Why would someone invest this way?"

The property may be inherited from relatives. They may have bought it at a great price. They may have simply decided to keep it when they moved away. The reason they are in the situation doesn't really matter. What matters is that you can help them solve their problem, and that can be your ticket to lower rent.

"How can I solve their problems? I'm not a contractor or a plumber!"

You don't need to be a full-blown licensed plumber or contractor. If you are even slightly handy, you could agree to handle small maintenance issues yourself. You can agree to deposit their rent in the local branch of their bank, eliminating the need for them to come pick up the rent. Yes, even with all of our current technical wizardry, rent checks are still a thing. You can agree to send them pictures of the property on a quarterly basis to put their mind at ease. You can agree to maintain the landscaping around the property. These minor services work to reduce the landlord's stress and cost of ownership.

Furthermore, think about what landlords in this situation must do in order to replace a resident. They must fly or drive from out-of-town at their own expense, hold an open house, choose a new resident quickly, and get back to their life in their home town. Perish the thought that the first open house doesn't produce a suitable resident. In that case they'll have to do it all over again - and again - until they find someone to rent their property. Therefore, continuation of rent is more important than receiving top dollar every month from a resident who calls them every week for small issues.

During my career, I've met many investors who bought rental property out of state. One California couple purchased a condo in Prince George's County, Maryland (a suburb of Washington, DC). The three-bedroom, two-bath condo was in a great community. Instead of facing foreclosure, the homeowner opted for a short sale. A short sale is a transaction where both the homeowner and their bank agree to sell the property for less than the mortgage. Most people are unfamiliar with the short sale process, and such transactions tend to be more complex than standard sales. But, the nearly 20% discount from market price was attractive.

The wife loved the chance to buy the condo below market. She focused on earning an "easy 10% return" with the intent of just renting the property and forgetting about it. The opportunity was more attractive because her relatives lived 45 minutes from the condo and could help her get started. Although neither she nor her husband had any experience as a landlord, they'd never viewed the property in person, and her husband did not want to be involved, she decided to move forward. They paid cash for the condo and thus had no mortgage. I specifically use the word "they", because once she bought the property the husband was involved whether he wanted to be or not. That's how marriage works.

Sources of frustration began to appear soon after taking possession, so the "easy 10% return" failed to materialize. Posting ads online brought numerous interested parties, but less than 25% actually qualified. They arranged for their relatives to show the property at a cost of $200 per weekend. Unfortunately, few qualified renters actually showed up. They eventually found a resident, but that resident stopped paying rent in the middle of the lease. The eviction process was 3 months long and cost $6,500 in lost rent and legal fees. Their frustration was ratcheted up even higher by a county requirement to spend additional money on a rental license to even access their right to evict. Completing this process only bought them the privilege of repeating their difficult search for a new resident. The level of frustration these investors experienced was high despite not having a mortgage and having relatives nearby. Without those two advantages, the experience would have been even more traumatic.

From this example, you can see how a reliable, dependable, and helpful resident would have made their lives easier. Renting to such a resident they would have gladly accepted an easy 9.5% return compared to the "easy 10% return" they experienced.

The power of proximity can be used in another way. Some states require landlords to provide a representative who lives on-site for properties of a certain size. In addition to the legal requirement, progressive landlords recognize the need for the on-site representative anyway. The role of this individual is to be the first point of contact for residents when maintenance issues and other situations arise. Very few landlords have either the desire or ability to live on their properties, especially if they own more than one. They usually fill this position by deputizing a resident for the job.

Who would a landlord choose for such a task?

In an ideal world, they would choose someone who already lives on the property and already is familiar with the other residents. This representative becomes a fantastic resource for them to get information about their property, allowing them to easily determine if a situation requires them to be on site or not. In addition to providing information, they might also provide access to pest control technicians, carpet cleaners, and other vendors. All of these services make life for the landlord simpler, easier, and less stressful. As such, landlords pay for this service in the form of lower rent. Since this strategy combines both the power of proximity and the power of relationships, it is covered more fully in Chapter 7: The Power of Relationships.

As you can see, there are multiple ways to use the power of proximity. When renting from out-of-town owners you have the best opportunity to use this power to your advantage.

The Power of Proximity

SUMMARY

❖ Distance can dramatically increase the financial & emotional cost of managing rental property.

❖ Reliability, minimal handyman skills and/or administrative skills can be very useful.

❖ For property owners, the continuation of rent is more important than receiving top dollar.

The Power of Proximity

QUESTIONS

❖ What simple repairs can you perform?

_____

_____

_____

_____

_____

_____

_____

❖ What skills do you have that could make your community a great place to live?

_____

_____

_____

_____

_____

_____

_____

❖ What help could you provide to owners who may have little experience managing rental property?

_____

_____

_____

_____

_____

_____

_____

Chapter 4:
The Power of
Timing

The busiest season for landlords is during the summer months. Everyone is working to get situated before the next school year starts. July and August are especially brutal and the asking rents in nearly every market prove it. Landlords charge more during this time because they can.

As they say, patience is a virtue and in this case that virtue can put dollars in your pocket. Avoid the hectic summer months at all costs. Look to rent your new digs in late Fall or even better in the dead of Winter. Properties will always have vacancies as people move out for all kinds of reasons. During the summer months, apartments are scarce, but during the winter prospective residents are scarce and landlords know it. As such, many companies lower rents in expectation of this slower period. That's why you can get better deals during the winter.

As a property manager, one of my responsibilities was to plan the budget for each of my properties every year. I won't bore you with all the details, but part of that process is to determine the number of expected leases that will be signed each month. The summer months are when leasing activity is expected to be at its peak, whereas these expectations drop drastically during winter. For my portfolio of over 200 apartments, my employer anticipated that my staff and I would sign approximately 45 new leases over the three months of summer. However, those expectations dropped to just 7 during December, January, and February. That's not 7 per month. That's 7 total for all three months. Just to put that in perspective, they expected leasing activity to drop nearly 85% during winter. So if you are looking to rent an apartment in January, you quite literally can be an oasis in the desert to a manager with a vacant apartment!

Furthermore, there is a second facet to the power of timing. As a prospective resident, it is best to look for apartments that have been vacant for a significant amount of time. In fact I would suggest using this phrase: "I would like to see any apartments in your community that have been vacant for one month or more." This indicates you may be willing to accept a slightly less desirable apartment for a better deal.

As I mentioned earlier, vacant apartments are bad news for landlords. Each day it is vacant is a day of rent that is lost forever! At some point, the landlord just wants to stop losing money and make something on the property even if it is not top dollar. This applies to smaller investors as well as larger property management companies.

Leasing associates and property managers desperately want to rent these apartments for another reason as well. These specific apartments continually come up in weekly leasing meetings as well as meetings with the property owner. Eventually, everyone involved just gets sick of talking about the same apartment with the same issues. Once the conversation reaches this point, leasing the apartment becomes a badge of honor proudly worn by whoever gets the lease signed.

These apartments may be vacant because the owner or the leasing agent wasn't properly trained. The leasing associate may have a poor attitude and other prospective residents have noticed. The property may not be marketed properly. The apartment in question may not have the best view or the best interior finishes. Maybe it doesn't get as much sunlight as the other apartments. The bottom line is "Who cares?" You are on a quest to shield your wallet from the ravages of high rents. All of these issues can create that savings opportunity you are looking for.

The most advantageous time to search for a rental property is winter. And keep an eye out for properties that have been vacant for one month or more. Your wallet will likely thank you for the effort.

The Power of Timing

SUMMARY

- ❖ The busy seasons are Spring and Summer.

- ❖ The slow season is Fall.

- ❖ The slowest season is Winter.

- ❖ Seek out long term vacant properties in fact ask for them by name.

The Power of Timing

QUESTIONS

❖ Are there any steps you could take to delay making a rental commitment until Winter?

_____

_____

_____

_____

_____

_____

❖ How could you make an apartment with a less than desirable view work for you?

_____

_____

_____

_____

_____

❖ Would an apartment close to the street truly be a deal breaker for you? If so, why?

_____

_____

_____

_____

_____

_____

_____

Chapter 5:
The Power of
Flexibility

Real estate is very unique in that no two properties are exactly the same. Every single house is different from every other house in some way. The same holds true for apartments, even if they are in the same apartment complex. Each one is different from the others. Obviously, one-bedroom apartments are different from two-bedroom apartments, and some apartments are closer to the street than others. But there are other differences, such as whether an apartment is closer to the swimming pool or the courtyard. Other examples might be how close an apartment is to the laundry room or whether it is on the first floor or not. Therefore, each apartment offers a unique environment to those who live there.

These differences stem from the fact that no two properties can occupy the same space. There is only one house on the southwest corner of the intersection of 5th Street and Almaden Avenue. The same is true of apartments. There's only one two bedroom apartment immediately next to the swimming pool on the second floor at the end of the building.

Understanding this concept is important when we think about what happens when people look for an apartment and getting the best value for their money. This search usually begins on the internet or by driving through desirable neighborhoods looking for communities that have apartments available. Regardless of the method chosen, you will likely have a phone conversation with the apartment community's leasing associate. Over the course of my career, I have had thousands of these conversations. It will go something like this:

Leasing Associate: Thank you for calling our apartment community. How can I help you?

You: I see that you have apartments available for rent. I'm looking to move at the end of the month.

Leasing Associate: That's great. We have a wonderful community with beautiful amenities including a swimming pool, laundry room, and covered parking. How many people will be living in the apartment?

You: There will only be two of us. But, we're looking for a two-bedroom apartment because we'd like to have a home office.

Leasing Associate: We definitely have two- bedroom apartments available. Would you like to be on the first floor or the second floor?

You: The second floor sounds good.

Leasing Associate: Great. Would you like to have a view of the swimming pool or would the courtyard side of the property be better for you?

You: A courtyard view sounds relaxing.

Leasing Associate: Would it be more convenient for you to be near the laundry room?

You: Sure, that would make doing laundry easier.

Leasing Associate: That's wonderful. We have one apartment that fits your needs. Do you have time to take a tour today? I'd hate for you to miss this opportunity. I already have appointments lined up for later this afternoon.

You: I'll be there in 30 minutes.

Leasing Associate: Fantastic! I'll see you then. I'm sure you'll love the apartment.

So, let's examine what happened during this conversation. The leasing associate is being quite pleasant and attempting to determine exactly what you are looking for. Their goal is to present you with the exact type of apartment you want. But, something else happened as well and most people don't recognize it. The leasing associate has introduced the concept of scarcity which leads to the fear of missing out. There's only one apartment left that fits your needs and there are other appointments later that afternoon. This scarcity has the effect of pushing you to act faster, increases the value of the apartment in your mind, and reduces the likelihood you will even attempt to negotiate.

From a certain point of view, this scarcity is real. The leasing associate is being completely truthful. There is only one two bedroom apartment on the second floor overlooking the courtyard that's close to the laundry room. They also likely do have appointments set up for that afternoon. There is no deception on the leasing associate's part.

However, from a different point of view, this scarcity may not really exist. We don't actually know how many two bedroom apartments are available, we didn't ask for that information nor did the leasing associate volunteer it. The community may very well have ten two-bedroom apartments available. If this is the case, it is extremely unlikely that ten families looking for a two bedroom apartment will sign a lease immediately, so scarcity would hardly be a concern. Each of these apartments is unique. As you answered each question from the leasing associate, you pushed more vacant apartments out of contention. They simply didn't fit the criteria you were providing. With each answer, the number of vacancies became progressively smaller until nine were crossed off the list and only one remained. If the person calling truly needs a second floor apartment with a courtyard view next to the laundry room, this scarcity is a true reflection of reality. However, if the answers provided were based on what sounded nice instead of actual needs, you created your own sense of psychological scarcity, which only exists in your head, not in reality.

Very few people actually recognize what happened in that conversation. The concern here is to avoid creating your own psychological scarcity by only providing the leasing associate with your true needs. While the apartment being a two bedroom likely represents a true need, the proximity to the amenities may not be.

For example, you may not need to be close to the laundry room, you might just need a laundry basket with wheels. Avoid prematurely limiting your options and manufacturing your own psychological scarcity. Being flexible where you can in terms of your desired options will leave you much more mental room to negotiate when the time comes.

Another area where flexibility can be helpful is the length of your lease. Property management companies love to sign leases and serve their rental communities. One of the issues they hate to deal with is when all the leases in a community expire at once. There are many reasons for this.

First, it creates massive uncertainty in the cash flow of the property. Remember, cash flow is what the landlord is after, so cash flow uncertainty is never welcome. While it's not likely everyone moves out at the same time, all the leases expiring at the same time allows for that possibility.

Second, it creates an enormous amount of work for the leasing staff to renew leases with so many residents at once. Meeting with residents to discuss their renewal questions and why their rent is going up is not the most attractive task the leasing agent has. But, multiply it by every resident in the community at once and they may choose not to come back to work next month. So now you're thinking "How does this benefit me?"

The power of flexibility can save you cold hard cash. While most leases are for 12 months, property management companies will adjust the terms of their leases higher or lower to help ensure that only a certain percentage of leases expire in any given month of the year. Ideally, they'd like more leases to expire during the summer months when rental prices are at their peak. Be on the lookout for leases with non-standard terms and significant savings could be yours.

Another example of where flexibility can save you money is related to renting in a newly constructed building. As mentioned in the example from Chapter 2, as buildings are being constructed property managers will attempt to secure deposits for apartments in their "new, hip community". This can be difficult to do as there's no actual apartment to see - just drawings (or renderings if you prefer the fancier term).

However, if they do succeed in collecting a deposit, there is an agreement signed stating which apartment the deposit is for and when the individual can expect to move in. This sounds all well and good, however anyone who has ever experienced any type of construction or remodeling project knows that there are almost always delays of one kind or another. Some potential delays could be the following:

- ❖ Weather
- ❖ The city/county inspector falling ill
- ❖ Materials being out of stock
- ❖ Unexpected permitting issues
- ❖ And many more...

So what does this have to do with me saving money?

The management of this newly constructed apartment community will be desperate for people to move in so they can begin collecting rent and start paying some bills. But, these delays likely meant the move-in dates in those deposit agreements are long gone. Since the original agreement has been broken, all of those people they worked so hard to get deposits from are entitled to a full refund, and are free to go rent somewhere else.

Alternatively, they can negotiate with the property manager to compensate for the inconvenience. This compensation could be additional free rent, a lower deposit, and maybe even free utilities for a certain period of time. The bottom line is the property manager wants to start collecting rent as soon as possible and make the community inviting for all the other people who may come to visit the community. In order to accomplish that, they need as many of those who left deposits to move in as possible, thus creating an opportunity for you to save money.

Be flexible on everything that is not a true need. If you absolutely need a twelve-month lease and must be close to all the amenities, then by all means insist on what you need. Only you know what your true needs are and what is optional. The more flexible you are, the better your chances of getting a great deal. Depending on the situation a little flexibility can go a long way. Flexibility on the length of your lease and the specific apartment you chose really can give you the opportunity to get the best deal possible.

The Power of Flexibility

SUMMARY

❖ Every property is unique.

❖ Make sure any sense of scarcity you feel is based on the actual scarcity of your choice apartments.

❖ Review the available lease terms for potential savings.

❖ If the property manager alters the original agreement for any reason, use the inconvenience to get some type of discount.

The Power of Flexibility

QUESTIONS

❖ How would you steer the conversation to avoid psychological scarcity?

_____

_____

_____

_____

_____

_____

❖ Would you be open to lease terms that differ from the standard 12 month option?

_____

_____

_____

_____

_____

❖ What amenities do you truly need your apartment community to have and how close do you need to be to them?

_____

_____

_____

_____

_____

_____

_____

Chapter 6:
The Power of
Household Composition

As a prospective resident looking for a rental property, one of the criteria that must be addressed is household size. All things being equal, the larger your household, the larger your chosen rental property needs to be. This is not only driven by personal comfort, but also by a general rental property industry rule. That rule is two people per bedroom plus one. The chart below shows how this rule changes the apartment size based on the number of people in the household.

NUMBER OF OCCUPANTS ALLOWED BY PROPERTY TYPE		
PROPERTY TYPE	BEDROOMS	HOUSEHOLD SIZE
STUDIO	0	1-2
ONE BEDROOM	1	2-3
TWO BEDROOM	2	4-5
THREE BEDROOM	3	6-7

As we discussed earlier, property management companies are much more likely to follow the rules than owners who manage their own properties. The result is that the options they present you will have the higher price points attached to the larger rental properties. One of the reasons they do this is that their communities likely have larger apartments to rent as household size increases. Landlords who manage their own properties tend to have smaller properties and have different incentives.

One of the potential advantages of a larger household is that it may be composed of more employed individuals. More working people in the household means lower monthly rent costs per person and thus more money left at the end of the month. Those who have banded together to rent property with a roommate situation in mind are seeking to maximize this strategy. This can certainly be an effective strategy provided everyone can live together in harmony.

The tip here is to use your household size to your advantage and not the landlord's. Work with owners who manage their own properties and avoid the property management companies if you plan to maximize this strategy. Look for those properties that have opportunities to use rooms like formal dining rooms, dens or oversized living rooms in non-traditional ways. Using this perspective should allow you to house more people without being pushed into the higher rental rates for rental properties with more bedrooms.

Landlords will be concerned about the extra wear and tear or the additional water usage created by having more people live on the property. They might want to charge additional rent for this, but this amount would certainly be less than the additional cost of stepping up to the next size rental property.

When I was working for a private property management company, one of the families living in a community I managed had a new baby join their family. As a result, the family of 3 became a family of 4.

Since they were living in a one-bedroom apartment, they approached me with the concern of needing to move into a larger apartment immediately. They were concerned because they were aware of the occupancy rules described above.

I was only able to partially relieve their concerns. There was no need for them to move to a larger apartment immediately. They would be able to finish out their lease in their current apartment. It was only partial relief because I informed them that the company would require them to move to a larger two bedroom apartment to stay at the community. The difference in rent between the one bedroom and two bedroom apartments was approximately $400 per month.

As the property's manager, it was my job to enforce that requirement. This did not sit well with the resident. I explained the logic from the company's point of view. An additional person would mean more wear and tear on the apartment and more water usage. It really wasn't a great argument since babies can't do much damage on their own and the additional water cost would be minimal. The other bit of corporate logic was that each additional person had to be treated the same whether they were a baby, a toddler, or a full grown adult. Unfortunately, my hands were tied in this situation. However, those managing their own property would not be bound by such rules.

The other household members we should discuss are pets. I know that everyone loves their pet. But, guess what...landlords know it too. This is why those who allow pets charge pet rent and /or pet deposit fees. Pet rent is a monthly fee paid in addition to your monthly apartment rent ranging from $25 to $75 per month for each pet you have, which translates to a cost of $300 - $900 per year. A pet deposit is an additional deposit amount paid above and beyond the regular security deposit. These deposits can range from $300 to $500 for each pet you have.

You might be saying "But wait, I get my deposit back when I move out, right?"

This can be true, but not always. Some landlords simply assume that they will have higher maintenance cost because of your pet and make the pet deposit non-refundable. Others may show the deposit as refundable unless there is damage other than ordinary wear and tear. Well, guess what? Fido scratching up the carpet or missing his puppy pad target isn't considered normal wear and tear. Furthermore, some landlords will charge you to replace the carpet in the whole apartment if they find any evidence of pet urine in the apartment.

The strategy here is to avoid keeping a pet in your apartment. No pet rent or pet deposit can be charged if no pet is present. I realize this may not work for everyone. But, if you have a close friend or relative who lives nearby, consider leaving your pet with them. By letting them board your pet, you could save hundreds of dollars per year in pet rent and avoid the required deposits.

If you must bring your pet with you, please be a responsible owner. Train your pet and provide the resources it needs to be successful. This will not only help ensure the safe return of your refundable pet deposit, but both you and your pet will be happier for the effort. In addition, avoid those communities that charge both a non-refundable pet deposit and pet rent. These steps will reduce your monthly rental costs and make everyone better off.

Working with smaller, independent landlords can allow you to make better use of rooms in non-traditional ways. This will prevent you from having to step up to a larger, more expensive rental property. Further reduce your rent costs by boarding your pet elsewhere or even just being a responsible pet owner. While the strategies suggested here won't work for everyone, at least you'll know about these issues before you set your heart on a particular apartment community.

The Power of Household Composition

SUMMARY

❖ Industry Rule: 2 people per bedroom plus one.

❖ More employed people per apartment means lower rent per person.

❖ Some landlords may charge a small fee for extra wear & tear instead of pushing you to a larger apartment.

❖ Specific pet rules differ from one landlord to another.

The Power of Household Composition

QUESTIONS

❖ How would you use a den or dining room as an extra bedroom?

_____

_____

_____

_____

_____

_____

❖ What additional amount do you think a landlord might want to allow a fourth person in a one bedroom apartment?

_____

_____

_____

_____

_____

❖ Who could I leave my pet with to avoid
   pet rent and/or pet deposits?

_____

_____

_____

_____

_____

_____

_____

❖ Would I even be comfortable leaving
   my pet with someone else?

_____

_____

_____

_____

_____

Chapter 7:
The Power of
Relationships

If you want to have any hope of your landlord ever cutting you any slack, focus on being a model resident. Pay your rent on time, actually quiet down when quiet hours start, and clean up after your pet if you have one. Landlords typically have some discretion over how stringently they enforce the rules, especially if they are small independent investors. If you follow the rules and get on their good side, you may not get charged that late fee. You may get a better renewal rate when it comes time to sign a new lease. The reason for this is that you are helping to make the rental community a more pleasant place to live and that helps with the continuity of their cash flows. If your actions make the overall community a more pleasant place to live, apartments in the community are easier to rent and people will choose to stay in the community longer.

While maintaining a great relationship as a resident is useful, you can reduce your rent even more by deepening that relationship. As mentioned earlier, many US states require property owners to provide residents with an on-site employee if their community is over a certain minimum size. For example, California law requires an onsite employee for any community with 16 or more apartments. While specific laws will vary from place to place, there's no reason why you can't use these laws to your advantage.

The benefit of moving from a resident relationship to an employee relationship can be powerful. The on-site role can be part-time allowing you to have a full-time job using the on-site employee role as a side gig. Compensation for this role is typically a reduction in rent which can be as high as 100%. Yes, it is possible to live rent-free working as a part-time employee for a property owner. With average rents across the US ranging from $760 to $2600 per month, it is easy to see the financial value of this strategy. However, this strategy also provides a fantastic opportunity to network because it allows you to meet quite a few people. While both of these are great benefits, this strategy becomes even more powerful if you have a spouse or a roommate who lives with you.

Earlier in my career, I met a college graduate who worked as an on-site property manager in exchange for free rent. His goal in taking this job was to explore his career options without the pressure to keep any particular job he tried. In the meantime, he focused on playing tennis, spear fishing, and selling cars he bought at auction. The role required 10 hours per week on average, for such tasks as showing apartments to prospective residents, cleaning the pool, responding to maintenance requests, and collecting rent.

After learning about the California law, he set out to find an appropriate on-site employment opportunity. He had zero property management experience and absolutely no maintenance skills. However, as a job seeker, he focused on what he did have. He had worked as a resident advisor in college and talked to maintenance staff on campus. In addition, interviewing people who were already property managers gave him insight into the relevant concepts, vocabulary, and duties. As he began to interview for these positions at smaller properties, he even bought a toolbox and some tools to help show that he was ready to hit the ground running.

His preparation clearly paid off. He spent four years managing a 20 unit apartment building. While in that job he was able to work in five different industries on a trial basis and network with prospective residents to sell a few of those cars. The independence and financial stress reduction this role provided was just what he needed to truly have the freedom to discover what his calling truly was.

If you play nice, then landlords and property managers will play nice, or at least nicer than they otherwise would. Taking the opportunity to deepen that relationship can bring massive benefits. If the landlord you have currently doesn't understand these concepts, then quietly start looking for another one.

The Power of Relationships

SUMMARY

❖ Paying rent on time forms the foundation of a positive relationship with your landlord.

❖ Make the community a great place by following the community rules.

❖ Always clean up after your pet.

❖ Potentially earn free rent serving as a property manager.

The Power of Relationships

QUESTIONS

❖ How can I ensure I pay my rent on time?

_____

_____

_____

_____

_____

_____

❖ What tools would make it easier to clean up after my pet?

_____

_____

_____

_____

_____

_____

❖ Are the community rules clearly posted where I live now?

_____

_____

_____

_____

_____

_____

_____

❖ What skills do I have that will help me manage a small apartment community?

_____

_____

_____

_____

_____

Chapter 8:
The Power of
Focus

Modern properties have added all sorts of amenities: pools, spas, playgrounds, beer gardens, etc. as well as courts for tennis, basketball, & volleyball. The list goes on and on ... and on. As a prospective resident, what you need to focus on is the fact that all of these amenities cost money. In one way or another, the cost of each and every amenity is being recouped in the monthly rent charged.

As a property manager, I noticed that there was a distinct difference in the importance of amenities when people were choosing apartments compared to their importance after they moved in. Listening to people when they moved in, one would expect serious competition for pool access. But, the reality was that while the pool was great for the online property pictures, no one was swimming every day. The pool did get occasional use, but most residents were really paying to have the pool as an option and not to use it on a regular basis. The takeaway here: only pay for what you are sure you need instead of paying for options you may never use.

So, the question becomes "Which of these amenities will I actually use?" This is important because whether you use it or not, you are paying for it. Seek out properties that only have the amenities that you know you will use. Fewer amenities results in lower rent, all other things being equal.

Something else to keep in mind is that there are many cities that offer these amenities in the form of neighborhood parks and recreational pools. These community resources are typically paid for with tax dollars. You're already paying for the community amenities, so why pay the landlord for those same amenities as well? These neighborhood amenities may be excellent and allow you to save on your rent.

The Power of Focus

SUMMARY

❖ Understand that the rent includes the cost of all the amenities.

❖ Know what amenities you really want.

❖ Know the amenities available in the surrounding neighborhood.

The Power of Focus

QUESTIONS

❖ What amenities are essential for you to successfully live in this community?

_____

_____

_____

_____

_____

_____

❖ Which amenities would be nice, but their absence would not be a deal breaker for you?

_____

_____

_____

_____

_____

❖ Do free neighborhood amenities exist? If so, what are they?

_____

_____

_____

_____

_____

_____

_____

Chapter 9:
The Power of
Questions

It is the job of the leasing associate or property manager to take you on a tour of the property. They will show you all the amenities the property has to offer. The leasing agent has repeated their script hundreds of times. They are cool, calm, and collected. They will do their best to put the most positive spin possible on the property. That is their job and if you are touring with a good one they will present their apartment community as the best thing since sliced bread.

Paying rent is not only about how many dollars go out the door each month, but the value you receive for those dollars. The leasing agent is a good source of information, but current residents are even better. Look for opportunities to speak with them during your property tour. Current residents have already taken the plunge and in no uncertain terms will tell you the good, the bad, and the ugly of living at their property. Do they repair maintenance issues in a timely manner? Ask a current resident. Are quiet hours really quiet? Ask a current resident. What is the quality of the relationship between management and the residents? Ask a current resident.

It is not the current resident's job to spin the truth for you. Once they signed the lease, they're committed regardless of what you do. You'll likely first meet residents during your tour of the property with the leasing agent. Keep an eye on the leasing agent while you have this conversation. If they're calm and relaxed, this likely means they've done the work to have great resident relations and you have a better chance at getting the value you're paying for. If they look concerned, agitated, or annoyed, you'd best be on the lookout for problems during the rest of the tour. It would be best to circle back to the resident afterwards without the leasing associate to be sure you got the full story.

Questions can be very powerful. In Chapter 2, we discussed the concept that some available deals reduce the upfront cost, while others reduce the monthly cost. If the deal presented is not the most advantageous for you, ask if you can get the same value in a better form.

For example, let's assume you need help pulling together your first month's rent and deposit. Let's also assume the rental community is offering $50 off per month with a 12 month lease. Ask if you can get the $600 off upfront (12 months x $50 = $600). That way you can make use of the deal in a way that helps you the most and the cost to the apartment community is essentially the same. I have seen this one question make the difference in many situations.

Another question you should ask is related to the concept of pets under the Power of Household Composition. There are some pets for which landlords do not charge pet rent or pet deposit. So be sure to ask the leasing agent.

Asking questions is a fantastic way to make sure you get the best value. Never assume that the landlord or leasing agent would offer these options if they were available. These professionals have so many things on their mind that they may not truly focus on your situation. If you get them focused by asking questions you may be able to have your cake and eat it too.

The Power of Questions

SUMMARY

❖ Current residents are an excellent source of information.

❖ Be sure to ask about rearranging any deals offered to fit your situation.

❖ Don't assume your pet will require additional deposits or fees, be sure to ask.

The Power of Questions

QUESTIONS

❖ How would you approach a current
resident to ask questions?

_____

_____

_____

_____

_____

_____

❖ What questions would you want to
ask?

_____

_____

_____

_____

_____

_____

❖ What advantages would there be to speaking with more than one resident?

_____

_____

_____

_____

_____

_____

_____

Chapter 10:
The Power of
Accounting

I know accounting can seem boring, but a small amount of accounting knowledge can go a long way...so stay with me. Rent is not the only place you can save money. When you sign a lease, you also agree to provide a security deposit. This deposit can be as high as two months' rent or more depending on the local laws. It is a significant amount of money that you plan on getting back. So knowing the rules about how these funds are used is important. The security deposit is your money that the landlord is holding to ensure that the property is not damaged beyond normal wear and tear.

When assessing normal wear and tear, landlords have to consider the concept of "useful life", which is the amount of time it is assumed that something will last. I'll use paint and carpet as examples. In my experience, carpet's useful life is 5 years while that of paint is two years. The specific useful life for these items can vary from state to state by law, but the key is knowing that such rules exist.

Enough with the rules...So how does all this save me money?

If the landlord properly follows the rules it won't. But, landlords may be sloppy or inaccurate and if you catch this mistake you'll save hundreds. I mentioned the issue of pet urine earlier and how landlords will replace the entire carpet with any evidence of pet urine. If the carpet is one year old, you should be charged for 80% of the cost of the new carpet. As a resident, you used 1 year of the 5 year useful life, meaning the carpet had 4 years of useful life remaining. Four divided by five is 80%. You should only be charged for the remaining useful life of the carpet. However, if you were in the apartment for 5 years or more, there would be no remaining useful life of the carpet and you should not be charged anything to replace the carpet. To repeat, after living in a carpeted apartment for five years, the landlord should charge your deposit a big fat zero for carpet when you move out.

The same logic applies to paint. If the paint on your walls is damaged in any way and you can hold out until the end of the second year, the landlord should not charge you to repaint.

Having this small amount of accounting knowledge can save you hundreds of dollars. Carpeting an apartment can run $1000 while painting can cost $500 or more. As a resident you want no part of these charges. In addition, this is another great reason to choose your rental well and focus on being a longer term resident.

As technology advances, property management companies both large and small are offering multiple ways to pay rent. Many of these more advanced payment methods revolve around paying with credit cards, debit cards, and checking accounts. These additional payment methods are great for providing convenience and for situations when actually dropping a check off is not feasible or is undesirable.

However, be aware that this convenience comes at a cost. Rent payments made via credit card or debit cards are charged a convenience fee. These fees can be as high as 5%. This may not sound like much, however average rent for a two bedroom apartment across the largest 100 metropolitan areas in the US varies from $760 to $2600 per month. This means the convenience fee for just paying your rent could range from $38 to $130 *per month*. I'm sure that you have more useful ways to spend that money each month. Savings, paying down credit card debt, or even going to the movies would be better uses. With very little imagination, I'm sure you could think of even more options.

So which alternatives are more cost effective?

Paying via a checking account is the best option. This method allows for modern convenience and usually carries no convenience fee. The landlord would simply bill your checking account directly each month.

Of course, this would require providing your bank's routing number and your checking account number to your landlord. Most people have a primary checking account where they deposit their paycheck and other income. If the thought of providing your primary account number to your landlord is uncomfortable, there is an alternative. Open a second checking account just for this purpose and transfer your rent payment to it each month. This would allow you to take advantage of this payment method's convenience without disclosing your more sensitive information.

However, paying by checking account only works for those who have a checking account. Large numbers of people in the US and elsewhere do not have checking accounts. Those individuals can still avoid paying convenience fees by dropping off a money order or a bank check at the leasing office or mailing the payment. While these aren't the most convenient methods, these low tech solutions may still be the best option for many people.

The key to this power is understanding that monthly rent is only one part of the cost associated with renting your new home. Knowing the rules related to your security deposit can help you avoid unnecessary charges. Knowing the charges related to certain payment methods allows you to choose the best method for your situation.

The Power of Accounting

SUMMARY

❖ Any damaged item that has served past its useful life should not be charged against your security deposit.

❖ Choose an apartment community where you would like to live long term, if possible.

❖ Avoid convenience fees when paying rent whenever possible.

The Power of Accounting

QUESTIONS

❖ How long is the legal useful life of carpet and paint where you live?

_____

_____

_____

_____

_____

_____

❖ What plans can you put in place to avoid paying convenience fees?

_____

_____

_____

_____

_____

_____

❖ What steps can you take to keep your apartment in tip-top shape?

_____

_____

_____

_____

_____

_____

❖ What steps do you need to take to get a checking account?

_____

_____

_____

_____

Conclusion

Many people assume that rent will be high and that's just the way it is. They are just plain wrong. You, as a prospective renter, have significant amounts of power at your disposal. Having just a basic understanding of how landlords think allows you to understand the issues that they face. Once you know what the issues are you can actually start to solve them. And solving those problems has value. That value materializes in the form of lower rent, a much happier wallet in your pocket, and a little less stress every day. It's the gift that keeps on giving.

Using these strategies to establish lower rent from the beginning may also help your rent remain lower in the future. Typically, annual rent increases are based on a percentage of the current rent. The lower the current rent, the lower the dollar amount of any percentage rent increase.

You may not be able to use all of these in every property rental situation, but the more powers you can bring to bear, the more likely you are to get a better deal. Landlords will happily give you these deals because you are helping them to solve their problems. You win, they win, and you can use this power with each and every property you rent from now on.

Thank you for reading Rental Secrets. It is my sincerest hope that this book will help residents and property owners recognize the value they provide each other. This recognition should lead to better, more fruitful relationships. I believe this is a necessary step if we are to ever address our current lack of affordable, quality housing. If you found these secrets enlightening, please take a moment to provide a review at your favorite retailer, refer your friends to RentalSecrets.net and stay connected to learn about upcoming live events and media appearances.

Sneak Peek

From my as-yet untitled book focusing on tips for choosing your next rental property.

All apartment tours are conducted during the day, generally between the hours of 9AM - 5PM. The leasing office will be open and the leasing associate will present the property in the best light. They will have practiced their presentation on the hundreds of prospective residents who arrived before you.

With the leasing associate on site, the property is supervised. Current residents understand that any activities which bend the community rules are much more likely to be noted while the leasing associate is on the property. So, in addition to the presentation practice, this is another reason the tour will likely go well.

You decide that this is the community for you and you're ready to place a deposit. But, you've only seen the community during the day. The key words in the previous sentence are "day" and "community".

Before you get your heart set on the apartment, go visit the community at night or better yet visit at night on the weekend. Everything can look great during the day, but it can be a very different story at night. This way you'll get to see whether the community respects the quiet hour rules. Maybe quiet hours really start at midnight and not at 10pm as the signage suggests. Maybe "extra" guests come and visit the pool on the weekends. You will have the opportunity to see how the residents act when the property manager goes home. You will also have the opportunity to talk to residents without the leasing associate looming over your shoulder.

Be sure to not only look at the community, but also tour the surrounding neighborhood. Will parking truly be a non-issue as the leasing associate suggested? Is the park they mentioned really as close as they implied? Are the amenities within walking distance resources that you would truly use? These questions and more can be answered by touring the neighborhood. In addition, there may be features of the neighborhood you would value that the leasing associate never mentioned. After all, you know your needs better than they do.

The information from your nighttime visit and neighborhood tour will make you a much more informed prospective resident. Renting with your eyes open is always the best policy.

Author's Biography & Contact Information

Justin Pogue is a real estate consultant based in San Jose, CA. His services are sought after by property management companies, investors, and real estate consulting companies alike. He got his start in real estate by purchasing properties on the Lands Available list in the state of Florida. Since 2003, he has developed and managed apartments, rental homes and student housing across the United States. Justin holds a degree in Economics from The Wharton School at the University of Pennsylvania, as well as an MBA from The Darden School at the University of Virginia. As a San Jose native, he also attended Bellarmine College Preparatory and the Harker School.

Network with Justin at:
RentalSecrets.net
Justin@RentalSecrets.net
Linkedin.com/in/justincpogue

NOTES

NOTES

NOTES

_____

_____

_____

_____

_____

_____

_____

_____

_____

_____

_____

_____

_____

_____

_____

_____

_____

NOTES